TO BE
SEVENTEEN
IN ISRAEL

To Be Seventeen in Israel

THROUGH THE EYES OF AN AMERICAN TEENAGER

BY JOSH CLAYTON-FELT

1989

FRANKLIN WATTS/1987
NEW YORK/LONDON/TORONTO/SYDNEY

Photographs courtesy of:
Israel Ministry of Tourism: pp. 16, 26;
the author: pp. 18, 19, 22, 29, 30,
31, 33, 35, 36, 40, 44, 49, 52, 54, 56,
59, 60, 65, 71, 77, 79, 82, 90, 92;
Hadassah Archives: pp. 20, 42, 43;
© 1986 David Dinerstein: p. 27;
Ann Chwatsky/Art Resource, New York: p. 46;
Stanley Newfield/Art Resource, New York: p. 50.

Library of Congress Cataloging-in-Publication Data

Clayton-Felt, Josh.
To be seventeen in Israel.

Includes index.
Summary: Provides a view of Israeli society through the
eyes of a visiting seventeen-year-old American, describing
family life, schools, the army, recreation, and other aspects.
1. Youth—Israel—Juvenile literature. 2. Israel—
Social life and customs—Juvenile literature.
[1. Israel—Social life and customs] I. Title.
HQ799.I7C59 1987   306'.095694   86–24723
ISBN 0-531-10249-1

CONTENTS

Introduction 11

One
The Setting 15

Two
Families 25

Three
School 38

Four
The Army 48

Five
Ideas about the Future 63

Six
Friends, Leisure Time, and Life-style 67

Seven
Conclusion 88

Index 95

ACKNOWLEDGMENTS

*Many people made my experiences
in Israel possible, and I want to
thank all of them: our friends,
the Harmans—Dorothy, David,
Danna, Oren, and little Milo—
for introducing me to Israel;
the Israel Program Center of the
Combined Jewish Philanthropies
of Boston, for creating the
20/20 program; the Cambridge School
of Weston, for understanding
that travel and off-campus work
can be educational; Grandma Sylvia,
for financial support; all my
grandparents and parents, for
encouraging me and listening with
love to endless criticism about
our lives here; and the Amars—
Etti, Armand, Itzik, and Carmi—
for being my family in Israel.*

TO BE
SEVENTEEN
IN ISRAEL

INTRODUCTION

I have been to Israel three times. The first time was a ten-day visit with my family when I was fifteen. I went again last summer when I was seventeen for a six-week program called 20/20, in which twenty Americans, ages sixteen to eighteen, went to a "renewal project" (poor neighborhood) in Israel. We paired up with twenty Israelis, worked together on improving neighborhood facilities, and then traveled together. Just recently, I went back to Israel for five weeks as part of my school's off-campus independent study program. I took photographs, conducted interviews, and lived, to a great extent, the daily life of an Israeli teenager. I lived with a family in Herzliyya, a town on the Mediterannean Sea, about a fifteen-minute drive from Tel Aviv.

I took this trip partly to visit the friends I had made the summer before, and partly to explore something I had been thinking about since that summer. The teenagers I met in Israel seemed different from the teenagers I knew in America—different in how they acted, how

ISRAEL AND OCCUPIED TERRITORY

Golan Heights

MEDITERRANEAN SEA

Herzliyya

West Bank

Gaza Strip

I S R A E L

Sinai Peninsula

1981

they related to each other, the way they spent their time, and their attitudes toward life. I felt it would be interesting to try to show and explain to people in the United States how life differs in Israel. Rather than attempt to discuss all of Israeli society and its conflicts, tensions, cultures, and people, I wanted to center on just one part of Israeli society—its teenagers—because that is what I am, and, therefore, what I find most interesting.

The particular area that I lived in, Shaviv, Herzliyya, is a blue-collar neighborhood. It is inland and quite different from the Mediterranean resort that people think of when they hear "Herzliyya." My "family" lived in a high-rise housing project. I live in a middle-class world in America, so the comparison was an interesting study of life for me. I also talked with middle-class Israeli teenagers to check that the differences I felt were not only class differences.

When I talk to people about some of the differences I saw between life in America and life in Israel, they sometimes say things like, "That's just a class differ-ence. If you lived in a small rural town in America, you'd see the same thing" (even though Shaviv is in the center of a city), or "That's just like America thirty years ago." As I mentioned before, I did talk to middle-class Israeli teenagers too, and they did agree with many of the things said by my friends in Shaviv. How-ever, this is not really important. The main point of my book is not to say what is responsible for the differ-ences, or that one country is better than another. I simply want to describe a way of life that is interesting and exciting to me.

I do want to stress that the observations and com-parisons are personal ones; what I've said about both Israeli and American teenagers are my subjective views and may differ from someone else's.

TURKEY

CRETE

MEDITERRANEAN

SEA

CYPRUS

SYRIA

LEBANON

ISRAEL

IRAQ

Gaza

JORDAN

Suez

Gulf of Aqaba

LIBYA

EGYPT

SAUDI
ARABIA

R
E
D

S
E
A

Nile River

S U D A N

ETHIOPIA

ISRAEL AND
SURROUNDING
COUNTRIES

One

THE SETTING

Israel is a thirty-nine-year-old nation whose bordering countries are Egypt, Lebanon, Jordan, and Syria, and whose water masses are the Mediterannean Sea, the Dead Sea, the Sea of Galilee (Lake Kinneret is its Israeli name), and the Red Sea. It is a small country, often compared in size to New Jersey. It takes only five or six hours to make it across Israel, traveling between its two furthest points—from Tiberias in the north, a green, rocky place where people hike past waterfalls and springs to swim and fish in Lake Kinneret, to Eilat on the Red Sea in the south, where young people hang out, get tan, sleep on the beach, and play guitars.

Although Israel is small, it has many different climates. In summer, it is hot everywhere—hottest in the south, Eilat, and in the desert—but in winter, it snows in the north and there is even skiing at Mount Hermon, yet there is still beach weather in Eilat. Sometimes it snows a little in Jerusalem, but in Herzliyya, where I lived, snow is very unlikely.

The country of Israel may be new, but the culture is old. Hebrew is the language of Israel, the same language in which the Old Testament was written. I have been told that the stone used for any type of building in Jerusalem must be, by law, "Jerusalem stone," the same stone used 3,000 years ago to build the first temple. This law exists because Israelis want to preserve the look of Jerusalem and not have it look like every other city in the world.

There are over three million Jews in Israel, and they come from every part of the world: Russia, Turkey, Morocco, Romania, France, England, America, China, Ethiopia, Syria. Together they create an incredible gathering of people of different cultures, clothing styles, looks, food, and customs. My friend, Itzik, for example, is the son of a Romanian mother and a Moroccan father. Itzik can speak a little French and some Romanian, as well as English and Hebrew. There are also over half a million Arabs, Druse, and Christians in Israel, and they add to the enormous variety of culture. Many of the people are very beautiful and very dark. Some look right out of biblical times, and some look right out of *Vogue*. Every Israeli has an interesting story about how his or her family ended up in Israel.

Some readers may think that when I said it takes five or six hours to cross Israel, I meant traveling by camel, starving in the desert, dying for water. Actually, Israel has cars, big businesses, hotels, high-rise apartment buildings, single-family homes, condominiums, radios, stereos, television sets, movies, music videos, dancing clubs, pubs, public buses, taxis, highways,

Skiing at Mount Hermon
on the Golan Heights.
Israel has a varied climate.

The Wailing Wall in Jerusalem and,
behind it, the Moslem Dome of the Rock

*One sees parts of the
old city everywhere.*

*A group of young people visiting
an old Roman amphitheater*

beaches, big schools, seven universities, big cities, grocery markets, shopping malls, high fashion, models, concerts, basketball, surfing, tennis, soccer.

In most ways, Israel is a modern place, but it has a way of making you feel in touch with the past. You walk by 2,000-year-old buildings now being excavated, ancient synagogues, and mosques; you see Hasidic Jews in their long, black coats; Eastern Orthodox priests in robes; Arab shopkeepers in their *keffiyehs*. You hear the Middle-Eastern music and smell and sample foods such as falafel, a spicy mash of deep-fried chick peas served in pita bread, which you can buy at outdoor markets or at modern gas stations. You go to the open alleys of the old market and find crafts that have been sold for thousands of years—necklaces and earrings and inscribed tiles—next to modern shirts and shoes. You are expected to haggle over the price, and when you make a big purchase, you'll be served a cup of rich, Turkish coffee.

Almost all Israelis speak some English and Arabic because they are taught these languages in school. Arabic is required. If you go to Israel, you should not feel shy about trying to speak Hebrew. People there are eager to help you and teach you words.

People who have not been to Israel may have the impression that there are air raids, attacks, the sounds of bombs and war all the time and everywhere. This is a myth. The border areas are only slightly dangerous. Within Israel, the major reminders of danger are the M16 and Uzi machine guns carried by the mostly college-age Israeli soldiers, and the signs on buses that tell you to "report any suspicious-looking packages." There are few real dangers. Israelis do not live in constant fear, primarily because they feel their army is extremely strong. I don't mean that the people feel *Israel* is safe. Most Israelis have lost a friend, uncle, or brother as a result of war or terrorism, so they know how fragile

*The Mediterranean coast in the north,
right near the Lebanese border. Israel
is in front, Lebanon in the background.*

life is. But on a day-to-day basis, they are not scared. War has not actually entered their country, and as for terrorism, that's a worry that does not change their daily lives. They do ask around if they see an unattended package somewhere, but terrorism is not something the Israelis I know think about a lot. I think that it is far safer to go out at night in Israeli cities than it is in Boston, where I live, because street violence is much less common in Israel.

Religion, which conforms to the Orthodox branch of Judaism, affects many things about national life, such as store hours, holidays, and when the buses can run. Although not everyone is religious, everyone is affected by the laws. For example, for the eight days of Passover, you can't buy bread anywhere. On Friday night and Saturday, *Shabbat*, no buses run and all stores are closed, even though this is the only time off from school when young people can shop. The Israelis I lived with were not always observant. Sometimes they celebrated *Shabbat* by having a big family meal on Friday night. Some people who kept kosher households would go to the beach on certain religious holidays. Although they disliked the power of the orthodox over their lives, they respected the Jewish religion. In America, a main way to feel Jewish is to be religiously observant. It seemed to me that Israelis possessed the feeling of being part of a tribe that they would belong to whether or not they were observant.

One of the major connections between me and Israelis my age was a common taste in and love for music. Wherever we'd go, we'd carry our radios. We liked the same bands. (In fact, Itzik and I had the same favorite band, Dire Straits, a British group that opened their international concert tour in Jerusalem.) The songs I played on guitar always turned out to be songs my Israeli friends knew, songs we could sing together. Of

course, there were songs I didn't know. They have
something in Israel called *kumsits*—gatherings, like hoo-
tenannies—where the people sing, maybe on a beach
around a fire, and the songs are usually folk songs
about Israel. Some songs came out of the Holocaust;
others come out of the different cultures that make up
Israel.

Two

FAMILIES

Most people in Israel are very loving. The first thing that the family I lived with said to me was, "You are our son. When you are in Israel, we are your family, your parents, and this is your home." Then I put my bags down and settled in. Today I feel that I have a whole other family, a group of friends, a home, and a world in Israel. This is how Israelis make you feel. So now I take you into Israel, into Herzliyya, into Shaviv, into my home and family there, to see and understand what it is like to be seventeen in Israel.

If you were to walk through Shaviv, the working-class neighborhood of Herzliyya where Itzik lives, you would see clothes hanging on lines stretched between the windows of concrete block apartment buildings. People lean out the windows, watching those passing by and calling out to friends. There are hundreds of cats everywhere. The streets and yards are full of trash. Torn posters advertising movies and elections are on the walls outside the small family stores found at the end

Herzliyya has luxury hotels
overlooking the Mediterranean
and fishing huts.

of each street. Though the streets are dirty, every Saturday, teenagers are out in the lots washing their family car.

There are always groups of guys sitting on one particular bench, talking, bouncing a ball, smoking. It's kind of like hanging out in American cities, but in America, I'd be afraid, passing by, that they'd start a fight. These guys don't fight, although they don't know me and they know I'm not from their neighborhood. As I get to Itzik's building, the younger kids yell, "Hey, Josh! Josh!" although I don't know most of them.

Inside the building, the lights are out until the second floor. Itzik's family, the Amars, live on the fifth floor. Their apartment has a small kitchen, small living room, and three bedrooms, each just big enough for a bed and bureau. The summer I was there, the Amars started building an upstairs living room and a terrace right on top of their apartment. By the time I came back the following spring, it was finished, and they were very proud of it. From the terrace you could see past Shaviv, past Herzliyya, to the sea. It is unusual for families in the neighborhood to add onto their little space.

Armand Amar, Itzik's father, is from Morocco and speaks French and Hebrew. He served as a paratrooper in the 1973 war and worked in the division that built the bridges across the Suez. He used to drive a construction tractor near Tel Aviv, and now he works in a market. Etti, Itzik's mother, is from Romania. She speaks English, Hebrew, and Romanian, and is a bookkeeper for an electrical company. Carmi, the younger son, is fourteen, and Itzik, who was my host, is seventeen.

To me, this family seemed very devoted, and I found that in Israel, generally, family life was much closer than it usually is in America. Ronit, an eighteen-year-old Israeli girl, told me, "Families here are very close.

Inside Shaviv

The author's family in Israel, left to right: Etti, Itzik, Armand, and Carmi

The Jewish holiday
of Passover celebrated
at the Amars

We are always together. We are like friends, and we always respect each other." Families spend a great deal of time together, and the idea that it is boring or a burden for teenagers to be with their families is unheard of in Israel. At the Amars', we would sit around talking and joking with Itzik's parents; neither I nor Itzik felt tied or held back from being with friends. Fathers must go back to the army for two months every year for training and practice; perhaps that is one reason why time spent together is appreciated.

An American girl, who lived with another family in Shaviv during our summer program, once said:

> When I arrived here, my Israeli partner's father was in the army. One day they received a telephone call from him, and it turned out he wasn't able to spend Shabbat with them. His unit was transporting a tank, and they were driving through Herzliyya, and he was stopped by the side of the road. So, immediately, the whole family jumped into the car and they all ran out to see him, and they took me with them. We just don't have that [in the United States]—you don't appreciate seeing your parents all the time. Even though they only saw him for about twenty minutes, it was very special.

Sometimes I would see parents comforting a teenager in front of his friends. A parent could talk about any aspect of a teenager's life in front of his friends, and it wouldn't be an embarrassing situation. Avner, a seventeen-year-old boy, said, "At home everyone is together, we take care of each other, so it is easier to be happy." I've also heard Israeli teenagers talk pretty freely about sex with their parents.

In America, I've never been to any friend's house where we sat together and talked with his parents for most of the evening. When friends in Israel visit each

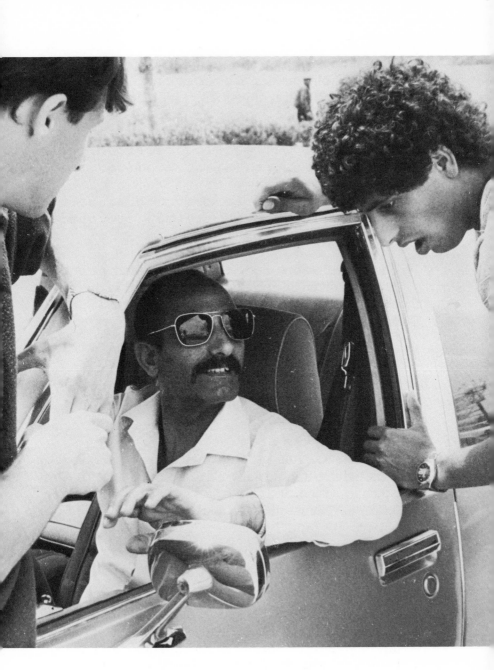

A father talking to his son's friends

other's houses, they hang out with the whole family. They eat, play games like backgammon, watch television, argue politics, or just talk. Ronit's seventeen-year-old sister said,

> I enjoy being with my family. Almost every evening we sit together, we are laughing, we watch television. I have friends who come over and we all sit with my parents and sisters in the living room. I like it when my mother or father is sitting and talking to my friend like she or he is her or his friend.

The conversations between teenagers and parents in Israel are different from the ones I've heard in the homes of my American friends, where a teenaged guest is usually just being polite: "Hi, Mr. Jones. Oh, yes, school's fine. Yes, I love biology." In Israel, friends often come over *in order to be* with the family.

When you go to a friend's home, you are always offered food, and, almost always, a place to sleep. "When friends come over," one Israeli boy said, "they treat the house like it's theirs, they feel free and at home, they feel like part of the family."

Kids will often go with their parents to visit relatives, where they usually all drink coffee, eat cookies, watch television, and talk. Itzik's younger brother, Carmi, told me, "Sometimes we just go for a drive with our parents. It's fun." I'm not saying that relations between parents and teenagers in Israel are perfect. I saw plenty of arguments. But relations are generally closer than they are here.

Itzik helped build his family's deck and barbecue grill on the new terrace; he helped install the electrical wiring in an entire floor of the apartment; and he always helped fix and clean the car. Teens in Israel do more chores—with their parents or alone—than teens I've

Itzik

Some apartment buildings in Shaviv. The small structure on top of the building on the left is the terrace addition Itzik's family built.

seen in the United States. I asked if they usually do these things because they wanted to, because they had to, or out of respect. Itzik told me, "Almost everything I do for my family is out of respect, not because I have to. Also, my father works so hard, so I help my parents when they want. You want to make your family happy."

Inflation and unemployment make it hard for Israeli families to make ends meet. Itzik's father, Armand, worked in a market because there was no work in his usual field, construction. When there were construction jobs, Armand sometimes had to live away from his family. He sometimes had to leave for work at four in the morning to work on the roads before the morning traffic; other times, he worked long hours in desert heat.

America is a nation that is supposed to be committed to family values. But I see friends who can't talk to their parents, and their parents don't know where they stand. It's as if they live in separate houses and meet for dinner once in a while. From what I saw of family life in Israel, spending time together as a family and family-type responsibilities top the list of priorities. Family time is also at the top of the list of what everybody enjoys.

Three

SCHOOL

In Israel, the school week is six days with Saturday, *Shabbat*, the one day off. When I tell Israelis that we have two days off each week, they are surprised, but they don't seem to mind their schedule.

There are two basic types of high schools in Israel. There are schools, like those in America, where you study different subjects and plan on going to college to experiment in more areas of learning, to begin to learn a profession, and to become a more cultured, experienced, and sophisticated person.

There are also schools called ORT schools (established by the Organization for Rehabilitation through Training). These are schools in which you study all the subjects, but in tenth grade you also decide on a profession to study throughout high school. ("Profession" is used to describe what in America would be both trades and professions—both "electrician" and "architect" are considered professions by my Israeli friends.) Then after high school and the army, you could either go on to college or start to work right away. In America, these schools are called vocational schools, and there is one big difference between those in Israel and those in the United States. In Israel, these schools are not thought to give a lower grade of education, and going to them is not considered to be lower class. Both types of Israeli schools must give the same test at the end of twelfth grade, called the *Bagroot*. It is somewhat like our College Board Achievement Tests, but Americans who lived in Israel told me it was much harder. A student of an ORT school explained, "The ORT schools are harder, and you must be smarter and work very hard because you must learn all the subjects they teach at regular schools, and learn a profession at the same time."

At the end of eighth grade, parents and kids decide which kind of school the kid should go to. Although it is true that more poor kids are likely to go to professional (ORT) schools because they can't afford college, this does not mean that middle-class kids do not also go to these schools.

Homework in the professional schools is often advanced diagraming and planning, for example, of electric circuits used in homes, airplane engines, or automobile engines. The next day, students actually build the circuit they had drawn for homework.

Ronit describes her professional school education this way:

> *In school I study architecture, and the army lets me come one year later so I can study an extra year of architecture. I also learn all the regular subjects like Hebrew, English, math, science, Arabic, sports, art. I also have one lesson (class) with a teacher, where we just talk, like friends, about whatever we're interested in. If I decide later I don't like my profession, I can change it after the army (or sometimes in the army). But to be able to change my profession, I must do well on my final tests.*

Itzik at school studying electronics

There is a serious problem with the professional high school system in Israel, and this is that it is, in fact, extremely difficult to change your profession after the army. In Israel, where it is hard to make a living, changing your chosen profession and spending a few more years unemployed is difficult not only because of the logistics and because studying again can feel shameful, but because your family is expecting the income. Where I lived in Israel, young people generally gave their salaries to their families until they were out on their own. Changing one's profession is in no way an accepted norm.

There are also army schools, from which many officers come. Avner goes to an army school:

We wake up at 5:00 A.M. to exercise and have an inspection. We study ten hours a day. I know this is a lot, but it is important. I'm studying planes for the air force. We go to sleep at 11:00 P.M. Because I go to an army school, I am all the time busy, but I like this, it makes life exciting.

I asked my Israeli friends if they thought that high school and college are important. One said, "High school is very important for the diploma, and it is an experience needed before the army. But college is only important for some people. I want to go after the army, but only if I can afford it. I want to go to college because one who goes to college is an important man."

Education has always been important in the Jewish culture. However, the views of these Israeli teenagers about continuing on to college are different from the views I'm used to in America. There are seven universities in Israel, but only about 14 percent of the college-age men and women attend them.

Since going to college is not expected, you are not considered uneducated or not well-rounded if you do

*Young Israelis pursue
artistic interests as well
as more academic ones.*

*A student arguing with a
teacher about Jewish-Arab
relations within Israel*

not go. "Only those who want to be scholars," my host, Itzik, said, "go to a university, because it doesn't guarantee any money." And it is not expected that teens go to college the way it is in much of the United States. Others had these opinions about college:

I don't think that people in the United States take college seriously. Some might, but it is just a continuation of school, there is no big difference. I think maybe some Americans feel, 'O.K., here I go, another four years.' With us, the big difference is that we have just had two or three years in the army. [So to put adult life off another four years] you really need an attitude of excitement and seriousness [about learning].

If I go to college, it is because I want to go, and I do the best that I can because it is for me. But I know that in America, you almost must go, or you won't fit in in many ways, and many people will look at you badly, and you don't have good jobs. So you don't go because you want to. Also, if we go to college here it is when we are twenty to twenty-five, after the army, so we are like grown-ups, not like an eighteen year old. It is bad that right after high school you need to do four more years of school!

Here, in some ways, the army is like your college. In college or in the army, it is hard because you leave home, you don't see your parents or family much. You are in a different society where you must start your life again. You must start to meet people, to know everybody, to make people know you and your personality, to be and do good—in the army, here, or in college, there, for you.

Israeli teens in their last year of high school are somewhat diverted from worries about their future, their

profession, finding work, or getting into college, by thoughts of the coming three years that they will spend in the army. What will training be like? What part of the army will they enter? Where will they be stationed? How often will they see friends and family? To some Israeli teens, the prospect of the army may take some of the pressure off achievement in school. It may be a break, a relief, and a change from daily homework and sitting in classes. The army gives many direct ways to get into the job world. If you learn a skill well, and show initiative and leadership in the army, it does not matter so much whether you did well in school.

Israeli students on a field trip

Four

THE ARMY

In Israel, all young people—boys and girls—must enter military service a few months after they graduate from high school, or after their eighteenth birthday. An important part of being seventeen in Israel is anticipating the army, and hearing stories about it from parents, older brothers and sisters, and on radio and television.

Men must serve for three years, women for two. The few exceptions include very religious people and conscientious objectors. There also are several other ways to avoid the army.

The army is called *tsahol*, which stands for "Israeli Defense Forces." All the Israelis I talked with said that it was very important to them that Americans know that it is a *defense* army. The wars against Arab countries have been in self-defense. The Six Day War (June 5–10, 1967) and the Yom Kippur War (October 6, 1973) were clearly wars of defense, but what about the incursion into Lebanon in June, 1982? As my Israeli friends have told me, when their forces went into Lebanon, they were trying to create a safety zone to stop terrorists

An Israeli soldier

Israeli soldiers at ease

coming in from the north. However, many Israelis feel that this incursion was a terrible mistake: "When we got there, everyone was cheering—they were so thankful for our help, but now they want us out." Israelis firmly believe it isn't typical for Israel to strike first.

There are many different sections of the army that new soldiers can enter. The soldiers have some control over which section they are assigned to. The results of written and physical tests, however, primarily determine where a soldier will be assigned. There are tank troops, air force, paratroopers, sharpshooters, infantry, border patrol, and many noncombat technical and supply jobs. Women usually have noncombat jobs. Whether you had a profession in high school and what it was can influence to which section you are assigned. Many people seek long-term jobs in the army. If you are an officer and you want to go to a university, the army will pay the tuition.

Most of our images of being in the army come from World War II or Vietnam, where soldiers were far away from their families for months or years. In Israel, even when soldiers are in combat, they are never more than a few hours from home. Some even live at home, and all try to get home for *Shabbat*.

When soldiers do come home, those who have guns bring them with them, with one clip of ammunition. Women carry guns sometimes, but not as often as men. Soldiers have to be extremely careful about their guns. To prevent selling or losing guns, the penalties are severe: a soldier who loses a gun can go to jail for three years.

The main question I asked my Israeli friends was how they felt about having to join the army. I found that some want to join, others don't. Most don't mind because they feel that it is their turn, when the time comes, to protect what their grandparents, parents, and

An old building with bullet holes from past wars

brothers and sisters have fought to protect so that they could be safe. But all people are somewhat scared, especially right before they go. The stories they have heard about training go through their heads, and they don't know what they themselves will face or how hard it will be. Also, three years is a long time to serve and be separated from friends.

Boy, seventeen:
> When you are seventeen and about to go to the army, you are scared. You start a new life in the army. You must be and act older. It's another side of your life— you're a big man when you're in the army because you're on your own, suddenly, without your parents. Once you're in the army, it's fine, but just before you go, you are scared.

Girl, seventeen:
> The army makes you grow up. It is a stage of life that every Israeli teenager must go through, and that we will all have experiences and stories from.

Boy, seventeen:
> I always knew that after school, I would have to go to the army, so it is no surprise, it's not too bad. Israel isn't usually involved in war, and then, the army can be fun, filled with experiences. [Working with people from different backgrounds, making new friends, developing skills.]

Boy, seventeen:
> Once you're in the army, your parents really treat you like you're a complete adult. In the army, you come home every day, or once a week, or once every two or three weeks. If you come home only once a month, it is terrible.

*Soldiers near the bus
station in Tel Aviv*

The fact that a few weeks seems to these teens to be a really long time to be away from home and on their own shows how close their family life is.

Boy, sixteen:
> *There can be a big problem . . . because we have to go to the army. Some don't want to go so they make a lot of trouble for the army, and some of them go to jail, but they don't have a good life after that.*

There is also tremendous guilt if you don't help protect your land and your people, who have many times given their lives so that you could be safe.

Boy, seventeen:
> *I want to be in the army because I feel a responsibility. It's my land. I must go, not because I have to, but because I feel it's important that I go.*

Girl, eighteen (in the army ten months now):
> *I wanted to go to the army for my country. I don't love the army. It gets boring sometimes; however, I'm not disappointed, I expected it.*

Girl, eighteen (who is going in the army in five months):
> *Oh, I'm waiting for this. I want it to be tomorrow! For girls it's so exciting—not to go to war, the army isn't all fighting. For guys it's good, but it's more fun for girls. [Army life is not as harsh for girls.] But, of course, I'm very scared about wars. When you see someone on TV who was killed, and his family is crying, and they bury him, then you feel so bad for them. But when someone you know dies in war, then you know what is war. It's so terrible, you miss him.*

Boy, seventeen:
> *I want to stay in the army, to make the air force better. The work I do is very interesting. I want to work on*

Visiting a friend
who is in the army

*plane engines, because this is what I love. Many times,
in the army, people get good, interesting jobs, something they like. So the army isn't so bad. In the army,
I'm going to be an engine man on airplanes.*

Boy, seventeen:
*I think it is important to go to the army here. We all
go because we must, and because we want to. We want
to have a country where we can have a good life. We
don't ask for much—Israel is very small. But we must
keep it safe. The army is very good. Every man and
woman in Israel must go, because you are something
special to Israel. You give help to the army and make
it better, make Israel safe. We don't have many people
here, so we must all go to protect our home.*

Although Israel is in the news in the United States
nearly every day—terrorism, Syria threatening attack,
Israeli soldiers being ambushed in Lebanon, and different conflicts with surrounding Arab countries—I always felt safe when I was there. You do not really feel
in danger, especially if you live there. Israelis feel safe
because they believe that the Israeli Defense Forces
would never let an enemy army over the border. Israel
has perhaps the best army in the world. But *everyone*
knows many people in the army—friends, family, young
teachers, and coaches—so the fear of loss is always
there.

While I was in Israel, a friend of Itzik's group was
hurt. He was in a convoy when a suicide driver pulled
up next to one of the trucks carrying troops and blew
it up. The friend was badly burned. Even though the
group had not known him too well, everyone was ter-
ribly sad. They visited him, and they talked all the time
about how he was doing. "Here you feel that even a
friend whom you don't know so well is family."

Boy, seventeen:

I have many friends in Lebanon now, and I'm scared for them.

Girl, eighteen:

I think there will be more wars because many people want this land. It is important for many people all over the world, not just the Jewish people. It is important to the Arabs, Moslems, the Christians—all of them want this land. But this land is ours, we've lived here for thousands of years. They can't come here and take us out and take our home. I'm scared sometimes because I don't know what will happen tomorrow, but I try not to think on this often.

Boy, seventeen:

If there is a war, I will go to help any way I can. I would help get people to bomb shelters and do whatever I must to help. I remember in the '73 war, the feeling is so awful, so bad. We watch television, listen to the radio, stay in the bomb shelter. In the '73 war, we were in the shelter three days, we wait for the war to stop. All the women wait for their boys and husbands to come back.

Boy, eighteen:

Nobody wants to kill anyone, this is the worst thing. But if it is to protect—to save my home, my friends, my country and family—then I must do it.

I spent an evening in Jerusalem, and in our small group was a young soldier. Since I was a guest, he took us out for coffee and offered us a place to stay, but he was very quiet all evening. When the two of us were driving alone in his car, he suddenly opened up and said, "I often just go up to these hills alone, look down on Jerusalem at night, and think about things, but when I tell my friends this they think I am crazy."

Helicopters go up and down the beaches, to and from Lebanon.

Ronit greets her sister,
home from the army.

Then he pulled out pictures and started telling me about his life in the army. He told me that no one knew what was going on in Lebanon (now called "the land of death"), but that he wanted me to understand.

He said that when he returned from fighting in Lebanon, he started to get on the bus to come home, and everyone was staring at him. He had bloodstains on his uniform, he was dirty, exhausted, holding his gun. He just wanted to be alone. He didn't want to talk to anyone, he didn't want these people looking at him. When he got on the bus, he noticed guys looking at girls, people arguing about seats! They were unchanged by the war, yet he was so changed. How could they fight over a seat when kids were dying in a war?

He showed me a picture of his tank. There was a big chunk out of it. "There were five of us in it, me and three others survived, but the driver was killed. I saw this kid, maybe sixteen, so I said, 'Oh, I don't have to worry about him, he's just a kid.' Then I look again and he's pointing an RPG bazooka toward me. So what do I do? It's just a kid. So I had to shoot. At first you say, 'Well, had I not shot, he would have killed me or someone else,' but then you forever see his face. . . ."

I should say that the army isn't like this for everyone. Most soldiers just train, come home once or twice a month for three years, and never have to fight.

Some people see problems in the army that don't have anything to do with combat. A twenty-year-old American studying for the year in Israel told me that he thought the army makes all Israelis the same, that the three years in the army break you down, that you lose your individuality for a while.

When I asked Shimon, a soldier who has been in the tank corps for five months, if he thought this was true, he said, "Definitely not. Of course, the uniforms are the same, but the insides are different. The army changes you, but that doesn't mean it takes your personality away."

Actually, nothing looks standardized about Israeli soldiers. For example, haircuts. I saw a soldier on the bus with a really fashionable punk-type haircut, and many soldiers have hair that would be too long in any other army. There is no interest in neatness, formality, or shined boots.

In everyday life in the army, the tendency to be in groups continues as in high school. In the army, people also have a group of friends with whom they always do things. Because you get the same time off, it makes sense to do things with friends you have made in the army, friends you spend two or three years with.

The army is considered a good place to meet girl-friends and boyfriends. Often, people meet the person they will marry in the army. You frequently see soldier couples holding hands and going out on dates.

The years everyone spends in the army often give them a start toward jobs and marriage. But after the army, where do their lives go, or, at least where do seventeen year olds see their lives going?

Five

IDEAS ABOUT
THE FUTURE

Most of the Israeli teenagers I talked with seem to have
a pretty clear idea of where their lives are going. For
those who go to a regular high school, I assume the
choice of a career is as broad as in the United States,
and is made mostly at the university. Students who go
to professional high schools have usually already made
their decisions about future careers by tenth grade, although they can change their profession and/or go on
to college. For students who do not wish to change,
once they are out of the army, if they have studied
architecture in high school, for instance, they can begin
working in architecture right away.

The clear and simple plans these seventeen year
olds seem to have for their future go like this: go to
the army; after the army, either go to college or start a
profession; get married and have children at a young
age; and go from there. Teens don't seem to worry
about money as long as they will have enough to get
by on. No one I asked about future hopes said that it
was important to be rich.

Boy, seventeen:

I'm very happy now [although he is poor], and when I grow up, I'll be happy as I am now and with what I have now.

Girl, seventeen:

I don't want to be poor, but I don't care about being rich, just happy, with enough money to have necessities and travel a little.

Most of the teens I talked to plan to marry in their early twenties. In my world here, many teens—both boys and girls—do not plan to marry until they are thirty. One reason for younger marriages in Israel may be that there isn't nearly as much divorce in Israel as here (the divorce rate is one-quarter that in the United States), so kids don't grow up with the scary anticipation of divorce. Also, it is not such a problem to have children early, if you haven't heard about or been in a family where the children constantly have to travel back and forth between divorced parents. There isn't pessimism about getting married and having a family.

One girl in my school here in America told me that she thinks there can't ever be enough love between two people to have them promise to spend the rest of their lives together. For my Israeli friends, who are often quite romantic, there would be no doubt that this kind of love exists. When I told them about how my parents had divorced and remarried, most of them were very surprised.

Boy, seventeen:

I want to get married, but only once. I think it is terrible not to be able to work out problems. I'd like to get married at twenty, twenty-two, twenty-three. I think it's wrong to have children and then divorce.

On the way to school

Girl, seventeen:

> *My dream is to have a beautiful husband—we love each other—and to have a beautiful home. It doesn't have to be big, just have a big garden. Just to be happy.*

In Shaviv, Israelis don't seem as concerned as teens in my world with creating their own future. They don't have to move away from their hometown or do something completely different from their parents to make lots of money. We, in contrast, must go to the best colleges, make lots of money, and plan oversize futures, regardless, sometimes, of whether that's what we really want. When you're seventeen in the United States, the first question someone who meets you is likely to ask is, "What school are you going to next year?" College here can be just more competition for popularity and status. There isn't much of this kind of competition where I lived in Israel.

six

FRIENDS,
LEISURE TIME, AND
LIFE-STYLE

The Israelis I grew to know have simpler lives than my American friends—simpler and very much like the lives of their peers. After the army, you get married, have a family, and start your profession. You'll probably live in or near the town where you grew up. Your childhood friends will be your adult friends. It's not likely that you'll change your social class.

Maybe it's because of this simpler, more homogeneous life that, unless there is a serious problem to discuss, discussions are simple. Many Americans want to prove that they are intellectual, well-educated, rich, and cultured, whereas Israelis seem satisfied and happier with a less complicated life. I sometimes think that a person in a large mansion here could not be as happy as the families in their small, cozy houses where I lived in Shaviv. Once, in New York City, when Itzik came to visit me, he was shocked by the elegance of the restaurant where we were having dinner. But when he began to talk about Israel, it was as if all the wealth around him faded away and no longer mattered. He got down to the simpler, more important things—family, the army, friends.

When you first look at an Israeli, he or she might look tough and hardened. However, Israelis have told me, and I have come to know myself, that this is just a front. Once you get to know them, you see that most Israelis are sensitive, friendly, loving, and vulnerable. Israelis do not put on an act with other people. They do not change their identities in order to be popular. Most Israelis will just accept you as you are, too. "Some girls or guys are snobs," said David, age eighteen, "but most are very nice."

I got the impression that teenagers feel they have to make the most of everything, love every moment; not wait for the future, enjoy the present. Yet Israeli teens act responsibly about sex. I did not hear of a single teenage pregnancy in all the time I was there. The constant awareness of the possible loss of friends or family might give Israelis a reason not to become close to friends, yet they do get very close. But an Israeli might think, consciously or unconsciously, "If I'm living a life of uncertainty, it doesn't matter if I smoke a lot of cigarettes, drink loads of coffee, drive dangerously, or don't exercise."

You can see that Israelis are definitely burdened by the troubles that confront them, but somehow they manage to be extremely kind, sharing, outgoing, happy people. Once, in Jerusalem, I saw a group of men standing in a circle. They were all yelling at one another, gesturing wildly with their hands. I thought there was going to be a fight, but it turned out that they were just yelling about the elections and arguing about different viewpoints and candidates. Israelis do argue; they are opinionated, especially about politics. Sometimes they seem arrogant. Whenever I'd say something Itzik didn't like, he'd click his tongue, as if to say, "How stupid!" But, no, it only meant he disagreed. It was annoying, but I understood after a couple of weeks that it wasn't done out of disrespect. Israelis have adamant beliefs, but they know how to hold them and still care about people.

Before you travel to Israel, it might be helpful to know something that Israelis do, so you won't be surprised. If Israelis have something on their minds, they aren't embarrassed to tell you about it. They will come right out and say it. Foreigners may think this is cruel or rude, but this is how Israelis are brought up. If a friend does not like what you are wearing, your hair, or how you are acting, he or she will tell you about it. And if, say, an Israeli sees a girl he thinks is cute, he will definitely let that girl know.

When I told my Israeli friends how open they seemed to me, they agreed: "People here are usually happy on top as well as underneath the surface." People you see on the street are not usually angry. "If you see someone you don't know, you don't give that person a bad look—you have things in common to talk about." Teens in Israel seem more willing to show their feelings, whether they are feelings of fear, sadness, or love. "We don't have to be cool when it comes to personal things." They are a loving and romantic people. In Hebrew, there is no word for like, only a word for love—*ohev*.

In America, it's rare that a guy would cry among his friends, but not in Israel. I've seen boys cry after family quarrels, and I've seen them cry after a visit to a military cemetery. When one of my friends fought with his girlfriend, he cried openly in front of a few of the people on our trip. When our American group was about to leave Israel, all the Israeli teenagers cried, and we, who had been changed by living among them, cried too.

Israelis seem much less concerned than Americans with looking "macho." Often, as a sign of friendship, guys will walk with their arms around each other and girls will walk holding hands. No one would say or think that it looks gay. People there can be affectionate and caring in public, and they can show emotion without others considering it "uncool." In America, being tough is being cool. Teenagers in Israel don't fight, maybe because they know what it truly means to fight. When young people have to go to the army to defend their home, they don't have to swagger and prove their toughness. Maybe that's also why they don't feel pressured to drink alcohol or take drugs to be cool.

In Israel, most teens are part of a group, formed during childhood, which, in Hebrew, is called a *chaver*. This group stays together for a long time—for many, for their whole teenage life, as a family would. "I would risk my life for any one of these friends." Individual popularity does not seem to be an issue. This group of friends is something special and different from what I have seen and experienced in the United States. It is made up of about ten teens who have known each other for a long time. They go to the same school and will be in similar professions. They know everything about each other and they always do things together. Usually, it is a group of all boys or all girls; if a guy has a girlfriend, she is likely to go along with his group.

"In high school, you have a group of friends who always do things together. You go to their homes and go out with them on Friday nights. Teens here are very close. We take trips together, and everyone knows everyone in school. The army makes us closer, because at our age we always talk about the army."

Friends in a group take care of each other. Once, last summer, it was the middle of the night and one of the boys had not yet come home. The police, called by his family, came to Itzik's house to ask if the Amars knew where he might be. Itzik went to wake up all the boys in the neighborhood to go out and look for him.

The group, or chaver

During my stay in Shaviv, I became part of Itzik's group. There are about ten boys who always do things together. Most are seventeen, a few are eighteen, and one just turned nineteen and is a year behind in school. He will go to the army at the same time as the rest of the group. There is Itzik, Yossi, Amir, Bennie, Avi, Shalom, Avner, Corby, Villie, and Udie. Girls also come along sometimes. They all go to the same school, most are in the same class for academic subjects, and many study the same profession. They have known each other for at least four years, and, in some cases, longer.

Itzik cares deeply about his group of friends. He always dreamed of visiting the United States and traveling a bit before he goes into the army this fall, but he told me, "I know that if I come, when I return home, many of my friends will already be in the army. Once your friends are in the army, it's hard to see them. So I'm not sure that I can come because I must spend time with them until we all go."

We have all wished, at times, for better friends than we have—more dependable, less argumentative, more sincere, easier to get along with—the perfect friend. I thought it would be interesting to ask Israeli teenagers what a perfect friend is. Here are some of the answers:

Boy, seventeen:
> *A perfect friend is someone who really cares about you, keeps secrets. If you need help, he wants to help you, or if he needs help, he lets you help him.*

Girl, seventeen:
> *My sister, who is now in the army, is my perfect friend. I tell her everything, and we understand each other.*

Girl, seventeen:
> *A perfect friend is someone to whom you give what he or she wants, and he or she gives you what you*

want. Someone you can be with most of the time and have fun. Someone who tries to help you and you help him or her. If you need or want help from your friend, he or she should always want to help. If you cry, he or she should be there to tell you, 'It's okay.'

In America, I'd always had trouble finding a friend I could depend on, who wasn't going to change just to be popular. I was particularly interested in Israelis' friendships; I could feel that they were different. The more I asked, and the closer I got to them, the more I was sure I was right.

I think I know what troubles most American teenagers. It isn't much different now from what the anthropologist Jules Henry saw thirty years ago. In *Culture Against Man,* he wrote:

> . . . in American culture, where no traditional arrangements guarantee an indissoluble personal community, every child must be a social engineer, able to use his 'appeal' and his skill at social maneuvering to construct a personal community for himself. . . . Meanwhile . . . others try to win his friends away from him into their own spheres as they attempt to build their worlds out of stones taken from his. Elsewhere it is unusual for a child to be surrounded by friends one day and deserted the next, yet this is a constant possibility in contemporary America.

All around me I see teenagers terrified of being unpopular. When I attended a large public high school in Massachusetts, it was pretty obvious from the first day that people envied or were looking out to be in the "cool" group, the group that treated everyone else as worthless. There was anxiety over being left out of weekend parties, being seen talking with the less popular kids. These teens felt they had to balance their real values with the popularity of those values.

In Israel, popularity isn't much of an issue. When I asked Israeli teenagers what they saw as their chief personal problems, they never mentioned popularity. When an Israeli didn't say anything about popularity being a personal problem, I tried, as an experiment, to push him or her onto it a little. The answer was always that popularity isn't a problem; they almost didn't understand. Below are some of the things they did mention as problems:

Girl, seventeen:

I feel bad if I say something stupid and hurt someone's feelings, because then I feel like a bad person. Or when I get into a fight with someone, because when I think someone hates me, it makes me feel terrible.

Girl, eighteen:

Once you are in the army, your life schedule is controlled by it, when you see your family and friends two or three times a month. You get commands for the first time in your life, where you must do something whether you want to or not, and this is very strange to some people. My other problem is that I have a boyfriend, but it isn't working out well with him. I was with him for two years, and now I feel that it is time for someone new, but I don't know how to tell him.

Boy, seventeen:

I'm unsure about what I will do after the army. Until you are twenty, twenty-one, your life is planned—school, high school, the army. But I'm not sure what to do after.

Boy, seventeen:

The main personal problem for me is that I am always worried or angry about the political problems, the sit-

uation in Lebanon. Also the conflict that we have with Arabs, and it makes me very angry that in my own land, I must fear the Arabs living here.

Boy, seventeen:
I don't have a personal problem. I'm happy all the time, really.

You're never angry, worried, upset, frustrated with the future, friends, or school, girls? I asked him.

No, really. I know it is hard to believe, but I mean it, no problems. I have everything I want and need, so I am always happy.

The last answer seemed strange to me. As for the others, perhaps their world confronts them with more serious issues and problems than popularity and what they are wearing or how they look. And maybe the anger surrounding Israel (three bordering countries still consider themselves "at war" with Israel) brings this small country's people closer together. The outer tension may bind them and make individual popularity something trivial and unimportant.

It is also possible that being in the groups of friends that I described earlier, you don't worry about your popularity outside the group. One guy said:

There is really no such thing as a popular person. There are groups, and one group as a whole might be more popular than another, or envied because of the closeness of the friends in it and what they do.

I think this is true, and, in fact, within Itzik's group there was definitely no one person who was considered more popular than the rest. Within the group, everyone was equally loved and considered.

I remember one guy who wasn't at all good-looking, but he had the most wonderful personality; he was friendly and treated everyone with respect. He was going out with a very beautiful girl. Now maybe I'm generalizing too much, but I think that many times looks are considered the most important thing to people in America. If those two Israelis lived here, they might not even talk to each other.

I found Itzik's group very open. They simply accepted me like a brother, and we all became very close. If anyone else wanted to come along with the group, it was always fine.

One person said:
> If someone new wants to do something or come along with a group of friends, it is easy because, here, people are open to this. We don't lock others out. But you can say in your essay that I feel that people our age in Jerusalem are different. If they have a group, it is closed. Also on a kibbutz it is closed because the kids there know each other all their lives. In Herzliyya, although people are welcome to come along with a group, different groups don't do things together very often. You just have your own group of friends who you are always with and can count on.

Something nice about Israel that would be considered impolite in many parts of the United States is that friends often visit without calling. It is not considered at all rude if you drop in around dinner time. You aren't expected to be ashamed, you are expected to join in. Itzik's mother told me, "I always make extra food in case someone comes over." An example of how much open homes are valued is a Morrocan Jewish holiday called *Memonah*. The name means open to everyone and anyone, and even more food than usual is made in case of drop-in guests.

Ronit prepares coffee for her friends.

When a friend, or a group of friends, drops in, the host is *expected* to offer coffee, juice, soda, and something light to eat. The host will bring in the tray of food and drinks, and everyone will sit around talking, telling stories, laughing, and listening to music. It is a fun, relaxed way to spend time for someone from the "you've got to run, be cultured, go out all the time" world that I know.

Friends here in the United States asked me about the conversations of Israeli teens, who live with events that make up our news: "Do they talk about the world and serious issues much?" Conversation in Israel usually revolves around an exchange of personal anecdotes, or other stories, told with humor. However, incredible intellectual ability and knowledge can suddenly appear in heated debates about issues of politics and money.

On weeknights, the group may all come to one person's house just to talk. On Friday night, the one night they don't have school the next day, after family *Shabbat* dinners, the group meets and goes out together. Where they go, of course, depends on whether they can get a car.

Israelis can get a driver's license for cars at seventeen; for small motorcycles at sixteen. Cars make a big difference on the "weekend." Bus service is good and you can go anywhere on buses, but the only problem is that they don't run on Friday night or Saturday. Unless you have a car (which is looked upon as "cool"), you really don't do much on your night off from school. You wait until the next night, which is a school night, to go out, and you just don't stay out too late. Without a car, you can, of course, go to parties, but if you have a car, you can go dancing, to a movie, to a pub (there's no drinking age in Israel, and not much drinking either), or just someplace where it is nice to walk. When the buses are running, however, you can go anywhere in the country very quickly and for little expense.

The typical Israeli car—small,
because gas is so expensive

If there is no particular plan, the group will often just drive around and hang out. When the group goes out and takes a car, everyone pitches in for gas. Almost every male is a mechanic. I was out with Itzik's group three times when a car broke down, and everyone combined his knowledge to fix the problem.

I asked these teenagers what they do in their free time. One responded:

I'm very happy with my friends. All the time we go to the sea, we sing, we listen to the radio, we go over to our houses and talk and have fun, we go to parties for kids who will soon go to the army or for birthdays, we go to pubs or to Tel Aviv. Sometimes I'll go out with a girlfriend.

What is particularly different about parties or pubs in Israel is that teens don't go there to get drunk. When I told them that, in my experience, teens often get drunk in America, they thought it was funny and strange. At parties in Israel, there is little alcohol, usually just champagne for a celebration. There is a lot of food, dancing, cigarette smoking, and talking, but little drinking.

At pubs or bars in Israel, there is always a music video playing and everyone sings along. In addition to alcohol, pubs serve french fries, colas, ice cream, and *hummus*—a dish made of mashed chick peas, served with pita bread. Pubs are a great place for friends to hang out together. No one feels the need to get drunk or even order alcohol. When Israelis do drink, it's just social.

I saw an example of how they treat alcohol one night when Shalom, the oldest boy in the group, had his nineteenth birthday. First, there was a small surprise party at his house. Many kids came over to wish him a happy birthday. Everyone gave him presents. When we went out, it was his "night on the town," the group's treat. The group made him feel like a king. We went to our favorite pub in Tel Aviv and everyone in the group, including Shalom's younger brother, bought him drinks. We all sat around drinking Coca-Cola toasts to him, singing loudly with the videos, and having a wonderfully hilarious time watching our friend get drunk. Although, yes, he did get drunk (for the first time), no one else in the group got the slightest bit tipsy. We were there to take care of him. After leaving the pub, we took Shalom home to his parents, who also thought his getting drunk was hilarious. We put him to bed, and then we all came back the next day to check up on him and his hangover. What is most important in this story is that everyone treated Shalom with respect, took care of him, and had a good time without being irresponsible.

It amazes me that there is so little drug use and drinking in Israel. In fact, not one of the approximately thirty people my age whom I asked even knew anyone who took drugs. Most responses were like the following two: An eighteen-year-old girl said, "Everyone here smokes cigarettes, but I never met anyone who took or takes drugs. I don't think people do it much in Israel. Maybe they do, but I don't hear about it." And a seventeen-year-old boy stated, "I know there are some drugs in Israel, but I don't know anyone who takes them, not in any school or army base. I don't think I ever met anyone who takes drugs. Here, if you take drugs, you really are crazy, something is wrong with you."

One person said that he knew that people could get drugs, but that was about it. When I told them that many kids in the United States take drugs, and not only marijuana, they were shocked and started getting the impression that there were a lot of complete burn-

Before Shalom's birthday party.
He is fourth from the left.

outs here. In the twelve weeks I spent in Israel, I didn't see one person taking drugs. Only once did someone tell me about a kid who was high, and this was considered very bad by everyone.

When I think about why there is no teenage drinking and drugs in a country with so much tension, I come up with three possible explanations. One, kids are given adult responsibilities early in Israel. Teenagers like those in Itzik's group, who go to ORT schools, choose a profession and start learning it in tenth grade. At eighteen, they are in the army, entrusted with what could be an extremely dangerous task—carrying a machine gun in public. Maybe treating teenagers like adults makes them act like adults.

Second, there is little fuss made over alcohol in Israel. There is no legal drinking age, and families drink small amounts of wine at home celebrations and ceremonies. Therefore, alcohol isn't that special, and being allowed to drink is not a sign of adulthood.

And third, maybe the security of the group helps. People are accepted for themselves, so they don't have to drink to be like everyone else. They don't have to drink to get into a mood where they can feel free or safe or say clever things.

Israelis do drive fast and offensively. They also drink a lot of coffee and smoke a lot of cigarettes. I wondered whether under their outward calm, the tension from the constant need for military readiness and the hostility between Arabs and Jews was relieved through fast driving and smoking. Once when I asked my friend, Itzik, why he smoked—didn't he know how bad it was for him?—he said, "Don't worry, everyone in Israel smokes. The life is hard here."

In Israel, there is another block of "free time" everyone observes, in addition to evenings and *Shabbat*, and that is around 2 P.M., after school lets out. At that time, all stores close, and it seems that all of Israel takes a nap. In fact, I once asked Itzik's fourteen-year-old brother, Carmi, why there are no television programs on between one and four. He replied, "They need to rest and eat, too." The seriousness with which he said this was hilarious.

Some Israeli teens do hold jobs in their free time. One seventeen-year-old boy told me, "Many of my friends have jobs. This is because we don't want to take money from our parents for things." Many teens work with their parents. If there is repair work to be done around the house, the family will have their kids help rather than hire people.

I asked some Israeli teens what they thought it was like to be seventeen in America. Avner, a seventeen-year-old boy, said:

> *I think that in America life is easy, but this is not good. Here, before the army, I know how to do many things, and, after the army, more. Engine work, build, repair home things that Americans must depend on hired or paid work for because either they can't do something or they don't make time. Also, here we grow up and are more mature at a younger age. Maybe because of the army, maybe because of our responsibilities, but I feel that we are more prepared for and happier in life.*

How satisfied are Israeli teenagers with life in general in Israel? Would they rather live in the United States? Here are some answers:

Boy, sixteen:
> *Many think America is the land of gold. I know it's much easier in America to make money, but this country is my home, it is something special. I want to visit America and other countries, but I never want to move from the area I live in now.*

An eighteen-year-old Israeli girl who has some American friends:
Americans always have to be busy, they always must do something involving money, and all the time they are coming up with ways to make money.

Girl, seventeen:
I'm very happy with my family, where I live, but maybe I would rather live in Jerusalem. It's a very special place—the people, the places there, the atmosphere.

Boy, seventeen:
I know we are not rich, but here all the people are like brothers, sisters, and family. Everyone knows everyone. All the time I'm together with my friends and we are happy.

Boy, seventeen:
I'm happy all the time because I do what I want. It's important to me to live in Herzliyya all my life because this place is very special to me. Here I have everything. I start my life here and all my friends are here.

The summer after I stayed with Itzik's family, my family and I invited Itzik to come to America before he went into the army. We visited New York, Boston, Cape Cod, and Los Angeles. He'd never seen a building over twenty stories high before, so being in New York City was incredible for him. He was overwhelmed by the money in New York. He was surprised by the fast pace, and he disliked the way the people he saw seemed so "serious," aggressive, and determined.

After Itzik's American experience, I was worried that he would feel left out, somehow, living in Israel, feel that he'd do better for himself in the United States and that everything was good here. But, when I asked him, a few nights before he left, if he'd want to live here, he said no. His friends, his family, his people, and his home were all in Israel. He said he might like to make more money, but to live in Israel was more important. I think he did leave with an enlarged sense of his own options in Israel. He didn't have to be an electrician if he didn't choose to. He could go to college when he got out of the army. I am concerned that his new experience may have caused conflict at home, but I am sure he will remain in Israel.

An Israeli man of about twenty-five told me:

The people in America are always looking for more and more money, and you may be more rich in America, but I'm more happy with my life than people are in America, even with lots of money. I go to work and make enough money to live on, and come home around 4:00 P.M. If I had children, I'd play with them then. I sit with my family, sometimes we watch television together or just talk, but we are relaxed and happy, not so rushed all the time. My life may be simple, and I don't know if Americans think this is good or bad, but I'm happier than you.

Many teens told me that they think Jews should live in Israel and are angry at those who leave. In fact, one Israeli told me this was his "main personal problem"— his anger at Jews who leave the country. They feel that so much went into getting a country where Jews were guaranteed safety, that all Jews should live there. Others, however, believe that Israel needs the support that Jews in other countries can give. This takes me to my next question: How do Israeli teens feel about their country? "Proud, ashamed, happy, angry?" I asked.

Boy, seventeen:

Of course I love Israel, I start my life here and I stay here all my life. But here, it is very hard to make a living. Maybe after the army, I will go to work at the airport and live near my family in Herzliyya.

Girl, seventeen:
> *I love Israel and I want all the Jews to come to Israel. I love the land, the people, and the way the life is going on here.*

Girl, eighteen:
> *I don't think I will ever leave, because I love Israel. It is such a little country and everybody knows everybody here. I want to travel all over the world, but then I want to live in Israel.*

Boy, seventeen:
> *I will tell what is something special about Israel, and why I love her. The people are very nice and close and special. You can go to any town in Israel and know someone, and you are always welcome to stay at friends' homes. Really, if you put me in any town in Israel, I will see someone I know.*

Some people said it is just too hard to get a job and to make a living with the incredible inflation, but most teenagers seemed to feel that if you can just be happy with what you have and not always want more, Israel is a wonderful place to live.

Seven

CONCLUSION

At home, looking back on the times I spent in Israel, I am sad because I miss my friends there, the things we did together, the country, the atmosphere. The fact that my friends will be in the army for three years will make it difficult to see them even if I visit. I talk about Israel all the time, and my friends here are tired of it. But when they heard that the reason I went was to do this essay, they all asked me, "So, where is it better to grow up—Israel or the United States?"

There are advantages and disadvantages to each place. In America, war is further away and America has no peacetime draft; Israel has always had a draft and has never had a peacetime, because its neighbors still consider themselves at war with Israel. Not only do teenagers there have to think about going to war, but at an even earlier stage of life, they have to see their fathers leave for war.

In America, it is easier to make a living. Inflation and unemployment in Israel make it much harder, and this obviously puts pressure on the kids in a family.

While there may be social tensions in America, they do not reach the level of tension existing in Israel from the conflict between Arabs and Jews, and from past and present wars. It must be hard to grow up with this tension and understand it.

On the other hand:

I honestly prefer the way kids treat each other in Israel. Here, kids are often so preoccupied with being popular that they don't treat each other with respect. They are afraid to show emotion, and many times they aren't themselves. There is much less of this competition for popularity in Israel, and friends are attached and kind to each other.

I think it is good that in Israel, professional schools are taken seriously and considered as good as schools that are only academic.

The things Israelis do in their free time are more relaxed and enjoyable than what teens do here. You can stay in one place and have a great time without "party-hopping."

In Israel, there is a feeling of permanence among friends. I'm *sure* that most of the guys in Itzik's group will hang around together as adults. I have the feeling that twenty years from now, I could walk into Herzliyya, find out where one of the people in Itzik's group lives, go over, and find them all sitting around as they were just last month with me. Such permanence seems somewhat unrealistic to hope for in my world here. Most of my parents' childhood friends live far away, and either they've lost contact with them or they see them only on special occasions. Here, it seems that we make different friends for each different stage of life. Of course, that's partly due to the mobility in this country that I do appreciate—we can change our condition more easily than can Israelis.

There seems to be less teenage rebellion in Israel, and perhaps this is due to the closeness of families and

*Four Israelis from the
20/20 program on the beach*

the fact that parents tend to treat their kids with respect and give them responsibility.

The simplicity of life in Shaviv was special, and the idea of having fun whatever you are doing was quite evident.

I would say that teenagers who have grown up where I lived in Israel are more likely to have had strong, stable family lives and a group of friends they can count on and not compete with for popularity. They can be themselves. They have a strong, tough education, but a pretty relaxed one. I feel that psychologically, it is a healthier and more stable childhood and teenage life than one where families move a great deal, and school and friends change constantly. In spite of war, terrorism, and tension, it may be the better place for a child to grow up in. One of the hardest things about growing up in this country is the lack of stability, permanence, and sense of community among friends and families. In Israel, neighbors, friends, and family can be counted on for many years.

Of course, the positive things about Israel may come partly from its problems and its needs. Israelis have something they must fight for and build, and this binds them together. In the United States, young people in the past often had causes to fight for—to end racism, to stop an unjust war, to take part in a world war against fascism. Now, there is little that ties young people together. The only problems teenagers seem to have to deal with concern their own growing up. The big issues, like the threat of nuclear war, often seem too overwhelming to join teens together.

One night I thought about calling Itzik, and, as I tried to figure out what would be a good time to call, I realized that I could predict what he'd be doing at almost every hour of the day. I suppose that predictability has its pluses and minuses, too. Basically, in Israeli society, there are more things you can count on.

The author spent a lot of time at the beach,
as do many Israeli teenagers.

It takes a long time to realize what's going on in the world, but it takes a lot less time in a small town in Israel. The experience of living with a family in Israel was fantastic. I learned so much about culture, not only about life there, but about life here in America as well. My dream is to someday have a small summer house near the sea in Herzliyya so that I can have the best of both worlds and continue the life I started there as well as the one I have here.

INDEX

Amar family
  Armand, 28, 30, 37
  Carmi, 28, 30, 34, 84
  Etti, 28, 30
  Itzik, 17, 23, 28, 30, 34, 35, 37, 67, 68, 70, 72, 85
Army, 21, 32, 45, 47, 48–62, 63

Dome of the Rock, 18

Eilat, 15

Falafel, 21
Friends, 32, 34, 62, 67, 69, 70, 72, 73, 75, 76, 78, 80, 89, 91

Golan Heights, 16

Hebrew, 17, 21
Herzliyya, 11, 13, 15, 25, 26, 76, 94
Holidays, 23, 31

Israel
  climate, 15
  culture, 17, 21, 23
  geography, 15
  inflation, 37, 88
  language, 17, 21
  population, 17
  religion, 23
  unemployment, 37, 88

Jerusalem, 15, 17, 18

Lebanon, 15, 48, 57, 61
Life-style, 32, 34, 37, 63, 64, 67–87, 89, 91, 92
  entertainment, 78, 80
  family, 25, 28, 32, 34, 37, 55, 64
  feelings, showing, 69
  food, 21, 80
  home life, 32, 34
  housing, 13, 17, 25, 28
  marriage, 64
  music, 23–24
  school, 38–47, 63
  sports, 16, 21

Mt. Hermon, 15, 16

Passover, 23, 31

Religion, 23
Ronit, 28, 60, 77

School, 38–47, 63
Shabbat, 23, 38, 51, 78, 83
Shaviv, 13, 25, 29, 36, 66, 67,
  91

Soldiers, 21, 49, 50, 54
Sports, 16, 21

Teenagers, 28, 32, 34, 45–47,
  55, 68
"20/20" program, 11, 90

Wailing Wall, 18
War, 21, 23, 48, 58, 75, 88

7989

306
CLA

Clayton-Felt, Josh

To be seventeen in
Israel

$11.90

DATE			
MAR. 23			

306
CLA

7989

Clayton-Felt

To be Seventee in

Israel